GREEN CHEEKEI

The ultimate Guide to a playful and

loving companion.

JUDY H. BOUCHER

All rights reserved. No part of this publication may be reproduced, distributed, or transmitted in any form or by any means, including photocopying, recording, or other electronic or mechanical methods, without the prior written permission of the publisher, except in the case of brief quotations embodied in critical reviews and certain other noncommercial uses permitted by copyright law.

Copyright © Judy H. Boucher, 2024.

Table of Contents

CHAPTER 1 6

   INTRODUCTION TO GREEN CHEEKED CONURES .6

      1.1 Overview of Green Cheeked Conures 6

      1.2 History and Origins 7

      1.3 Why Green Cheeked Conures Make Great Pets 8

CHAPTER 2 10

   UNDERSTANDING THE GREEN CHEEKED CONURE SPECIES 10

      2.1 Physical Characteristics and Varieties 11

      2.2 Personality Traits and Behavior 12

      2.3 Social Needs and Intelligence 13

CHAPTER 3 15

   SETTING UP THE IDEAL HOME FOR YOUR GREEN CHEEKED CONURE 15

      3.1 Choosing the Right Cage 15

      3.2 Necessary Cage Accessories and Setup 17

      3.3 Environmental Enrichment (Toys, Perches, and More) 19

CHAPTER 4 21

   FEEDING YOUR GREEN CHEEKED CONURE 21

      4.1 Balanced Diet: What to Feed and What to Avoid .21

4.2 Fresh Foods, Pellets, and Seeds 23

4.3 Special Dietary Considerations and Treats 25

CHAPTER 5 27

TRAINING AND SOCIALIZING YOUR GREEN CHEEKED CONURE 27

5.1 Basic Training Techniques 27

5.2 Bonding and Socializing with Your Conure 29

5.3 Teaching Fun Tricks and Vocalizations 31

CHAPTER 6 34

HEALTH AND WELL-BEING OF GREEN CHEEKED CONURES 34

6.1 Common Health Issues and Symptoms 34

6.2 Regular Health Check-Ups and Preventative Care 36

6.3 Ensuring Mental and Physical Stimulation 38

CHAPTER 7 41

BEHAVIORAL CHALLENGES AND SOLUTIONS 41

7.1 Addressing Common Behavioral Problems 42

7.2 Handling Aggression, Biting, and Screaming 44

7.3 Understanding and Managing Stress 46

CHAPTER 8 49

BREEDING AND RAISING GREEN CHEEKED CONURES 49

    8.1 Preparing for Breeding..49

    8.2 Caring for Eggs and Chicks 52

    8.3 Tips for Raising Healthy Baby Conures 54

CONCLUSION..57

CHAPTER 1

INTRODUCTION TO GREEN CHEEKED CONURES

Green Cheeked Conures are vibrant, intelligent, and affectionate parrots that belong to the Pyrrhura genus of the parrot family. Their captivating personalities and striking appearance make them a favorite among bird enthusiasts. These small to medium-sized parrots are known for their lively nature, playful antics, and ability to bond deeply with their human companions. Their manageable size, relative ease of care, and adaptability make them an excellent choice for both novice and experienced bird owners.

1.1 Overview of Green Cheeked Conures

Green Cheeked Conures are native to South America, primarily inhabiting regions of Brazil,

Bolivia, Argentina, and Paraguay. These birds are distinguished by their green feathers, which are accented by vibrant shades of blue, red, and yellow, depending on the mutation. They typically grow to about 10 inches in length and weigh around 60-80 grams, making them one of the smaller conure species. Despite their small size, Green Cheeked Conures are known for their big personalities, displaying curiosity, energy, and an inclination for mischief. Their quieter vocalizations compared to other parrots add to their appeal for those living in apartments or shared spaces.

1.2 History and Origins

The history of Green Cheeked Conures can be traced back to the dense tropical forests and savannahs of South America, where they thrive in flocks. These social birds have adapted well to their natural habitats, feeding on fruits, seeds, and vegetation. In the aviculture world, they were first introduced as pets in the mid-20th century and quickly gained popularity due to their affectionate demeanor and striking coloration. Over time, breeders have developed various mutations, such as pineapple, cinnamon, and yellow-sided variants, which further enhanced their desirability as companion birds. Their enduring popularity reflects their natural charm and suitability for domestication.

1.3 Why Green Cheeked Conures Make Great Pets

Green Cheeked Conures are celebrated for their affectionate and engaging personalities, making them ideal companions. They are highly intelligent and can learn tricks, mimic sounds, and even recognize their owners, fostering a strong bond. Their playful nature ensures they remain entertaining, and their social disposition makes them thrive in environments where they receive regular interaction and stimulation. Compared to other parrot species, they are relatively low-maintenance, requiring a healthy diet, regular exercise, and mental enrichment. Furthermore, their smaller size and quieter demeanor make them less demanding in terms of space and noise, making them perfect for pet owners seeking a loyal and loving avian companion.

These qualities combined make Green Cheeked Conures an exceptional choice for those looking to enrich their lives with a feathery friend.

CHAPTER 2
UNDERSTANDING THE GREEN CHEEKED CONURE SPECIES

Green Cheeked Conures are an extraordinary species of small parrots that captivate bird enthusiasts with their vibrant appearance, playful personalities, and remarkable intelligence. Understanding the nuances of their physical traits, behavior, and social needs can provide insight into what makes them such cherished companions. These parrots are not just visually stunning; their complex social dynamics and engaging nature make them truly unique members of the avian world.

2.1 Physical Characteristics and Varieties

Green Cheeked Conures are small to medium-sized parrots, typically measuring about 10 inches in length and weighing between 60 to 80 grams. They possess a compact body adorned with predominantly green feathers that shimmer in the light, giving them a vivid and lively appearance. Their characteristic dark brown or black heads, maroon-colored tail feathers, and blue primary wing feathers add contrast to their green plumage.

In addition to the natural coloration, Green Cheeked Conures are available in several mutations, each offering a distinct variation in their appearance. Popular mutations include the **Cinnamon**, which features lighter, more subdued green tones; the **Pineapple**, with vibrant yellow and red undertones; and the **Yellow-Sided**, showcasing enhanced yellow coloration on their chest and belly. These mutations not only add aesthetic appeal but also allow owners to choose a bird that resonates with their personal preference. Despite their varied appearances, all Green Cheeked Conures share a sturdy build and distinctive short, curved beaks that are well-suited for climbing, chewing, and feeding.

2.2 Personality Traits and Behavior

One of the most endearing qualities of Green Cheeked Conures is their spirited personality. They are highly playful and curious, often exploring their environment with boundless energy. This natural inquisitiveness sometimes translates into mischievous behavior, such as nibbling on household items or investigating places they shouldn't. Despite this, their antics are usually entertaining rather than troublesome, and they are quick learners when it comes to setting boundaries with consistent training.

Green Cheeked Conures are also affectionate birds that thrive on interaction and companionship. They form strong bonds with their human caregivers, often seeking out attention through gentle head bobs, cuddles, or playful chirps. While they are not as vocal as other parrot species, they can mimic sounds and exhibit a range of expressive calls to communicate their needs and emotions. Additionally, these birds are known for their resilience and adaptability, making them well-suited to a variety of living situations, from bustling households to quieter environments.

2.3 Social Needs and Intelligence

Green Cheeked Conures are inherently social creatures that crave interaction and stimulation. In the wild, they live in flocks, where they engage in communal activities like foraging, preening, and vocalizing. In captivity, this flock-like bond translates to their relationship with their human caregivers or other birds in the household. Without adequate socialization, they can become lonely or bored, which may lead to undesirable behaviors like feather plucking or excessive vocalization.

Their intelligence is another defining feature of their species. Green Cheeked Conures are quick learners capable of understanding commands, learning tricks, and even recognizing patterns in their daily routines. Their ability to solve puzzles and adapt to new situations highlights their cognitive capabilities. Owners can cater to their mental needs by providing interactive toys, teaching them simple tasks, or engaging them in playful activities like fetch or hide-and-seek.

Meeting their social and intellectual needs requires time and effort, but the rewards are immense. A well-socialized and mentally stimulated Green Cheeked Conure will not only thrive but also forge an irreplaceable bond with its owner, becoming a loyal and loving companion for many years.

CHAPTER 3
SETTING UP THE IDEAL HOME FOR YOUR GREEN CHEEKED CONURE

Creating a comfortable and stimulating living environment is essential for the well-being of your Green Cheeked Conure. A well-designed habitat not only meets their basic needs but also supports their mental and physical health. From selecting the right cage to including accessories and enrichment items, careful planning ensures that your conure thrives in its home.

3.1 Choosing the Right Cage

The cage is the cornerstone of your conure's living environment, and selecting the right one is critical. A cage that is too small or poorly designed can lead to stress and health issues for your bird.

A spacious cage is vital for Green Cheeked Conures, as they are active and enjoy climbing, stretching their wings, and moving around. The minimum recommended size is 24 inches wide, 24 inches deep, and 30 inches tall, but larger is always better. The bar spacing should be between ½ to ¾ inch to prevent escape and ensure safety. Overly wide bars can result in injuries, as conures may try to squeeze through them.

Material quality is another important consideration. Cages made from stainless steel or powder-coated metal are ideal because they are durable, easy to clean, and free of toxic substances like lead or zinc, which can harm your bird. Accessibility and ease of cleaning should also factor into your choice. A cage with a removable tray and grates makes cleaning convenient, ensuring the environment remains hygienic and free of bacteria or mold.

Finally, placement matters. The cage should be located in a well-ventilated, well-lit area, away from drafts, direct sunlight, or high-traffic zones where noise and activity might stress the bird. Avoid placing the cage near the kitchen to prevent exposure to harmful cooking fumes, particularly those from non-stick cookware.

3.2 Necessary Cage Accessories and Setup

A properly equipped cage is essential for meeting your conure's daily needs. Thoughtful inclusion of accessories will enhance their quality of life and make their environment more engaging.

Perches are fundamental to your bird's comfort and foot health. Provide a variety of perches with different diameters and textures, such as natural wood (manzanita or java wood) and rope perches. This diversity helps prevent foot sores and keeps their feet strong. Avoid sandpaper perches, as these can cause abrasions and discomfort.

Food and water bowls should be sturdy, easy to clean, and positioned at a height that is easily accessible to your conure. Stainless steel or ceramic bowls are preferred because they resist bacteria buildup. Make sure the bowls are secured to prevent tipping or spillage.

Add a sleeping area to provide your conure with a sense of security. This can be a soft platform, a small sleeping tent, or a nest box. These additions create a cozy retreat for rest and relaxation, especially during the night.

The cage's bottom should be lined with paper or cage liners for easy cleaning. Avoid substrates like wood shavings or sand, as they can harbor bacteria and cause respiratory problems. Additionally, ensure that the cage has ample lighting, either from natural sunlight or full-spectrum bulbs, to support your bird's health and circadian rhythms.

3.3 Environmental Enrichment (Toys, Perches, and More)

Environmental enrichment is crucial for keeping Green Cheeked Conures happy and mentally stimulated. These intelligent and curious birds thrive in an environment filled with opportunities for play and exploration.

Toys are a must-have for your conure. Include a mix of chewable toys, puzzle feeders, and interactive playthings to keep them engaged. Conures love to chew, so toys made of natural wood, leather, or other bird-safe materials are excellent for satisfying this instinct. Rotate toys regularly to maintain their interest and prevent boredom.

Climbing structures such as ropes, ladders, and swings encourage physical activity and mimic their natural behaviors. These items help keep your bird fit and provide an outlet for their energy. Adding perches at varying heights and locations within the cage can also encourage climbing and exploration.

Foraging opportunities are another excellent form of enrichment. Hide treats or food in foraging toys or create simple puzzles for your conure to solve. This taps into their natural instincts to search for food and provides mental stimulation.

Bathing options should also be provided. Many Green Cheeked Conures enjoy water play, so include a shallow dish for bathing or mist them lightly with water. This helps keep their feathers clean and provides an enjoyable activity.

Lastly, spend time interacting with your bird daily. No amount of enrichment can replace the bond they share with their human caregivers. Regular socialization, coupled with a well-equipped and stimulating cage, ensures your Green Cheeked Conure enjoys a happy, healthy, and fulfilling life.

CHAPTER 4
FEEDING YOUR GREEN CHEEKED CONURE

A proper diet is the foundation of your Green Cheeked Conure's health and longevity. These active and playful birds require a well-rounded diet to support their energy needs, feather health, and overall well-being. Understanding what to feed, how to incorporate variety, and what special considerations to keep in mind ensures that your conure thrives.

4.1 Balanced Diet: What to Feed and What to Avoid

Providing a balanced diet is essential to meet your conure's nutritional needs. A diet that is too limited or overly reliant on one type of food can lead to deficiencies or health problems.

The ideal diet for a Green Cheeked Conure consists of a mix of high-quality pellets, fresh fruits and vegetables, and occasional seeds. Pellets should make up the majority of their diet, approximately 60-70%. These are specially formulated to provide essential vitamins and nutrients. Ensure the pellets are free from artificial colors or preservatives.

Fresh fruits and vegetables should account for about 20-30% of their diet. Offer a variety of options such as apples, berries, mango, carrots, broccoli, and leafy greens. Always wash produce thoroughly and remove any pits or seeds, as these can be toxic.

Seeds, while a natural part of their diet, should be fed sparingly. They are high in fat and can lead to obesity if overconsumed. Limit seeds to treats or occasional rewards during training.

Certain foods are toxic to conures and must be avoided entirely. These include avocado, chocolate, caffeine, alcohol, garlic, and onions. Additionally, avoid foods high in sugar or salt, as they can harm your bird's health.

4.2 Fresh Foods, Pellets, and Seeds

Fresh foods, pellets, and seeds each play a distinct role in your conure's diet, and striking the right balance is key to ensuring variety and nutrition.

1. Fresh Foods: Fresh fruits and vegetables are vital for providing hydration, fiber, and a wide range of vitamins. Rotate different types to maintain your bird's interest and ensure they receive diverse nutrients. For example, offer kale or spinach one day and carrots or bell peppers the next. Avoid over-reliance on fruits, as they are high in sugar; vegetables should make up the bulk of the fresh food portion.

2. Pellets: High-quality pellets serve as the cornerstone of your conure's diet. They are designed to deliver balanced nutrition, filling in gaps that fresh foods might not cover. Choose pellets made specifically for small parrots and avoid those with artificial additives. Transitioning your bird to pellets, if they are not already accustomed, should be done gradually to ensure acceptance.

3. Seeds: Seeds are a favorite of conures, but they should be viewed as a treat rather than a staple. While seeds like millet or sunflower provide energy, their high fat content makes them unsuitable as a primary food source. Use seeds to reward good behavior or mix them sparingly with pellets to add variety.

By combining fresh foods, pellets, and seeds in the right proportions, you can create a nutritionally complete and enjoyable diet for your Green Cheeked Conure.

4.3 Special Dietary Considerations and Treats

Green Cheeked Conures may have special dietary needs based on their age, activity level, or health. Additionally, treats can be used strategically to enhance their diet and training.

1. Special Considerations: Young conures, during their growing phase, require more protein to support their development. This can be provided through small amounts of cooked eggs or legumes.

Older birds, on the other hand, may benefit from foods rich in antioxidants, like blueberries, to support their immune system. Birds with specific health conditions, such as obesity or feather plucking, may need specialized diets guided by a veterinarian.

2. Treats: Treats are an excellent way to bond with your conure and reinforce training. Offer healthy options like unsalted nuts, small pieces of fruit, or store-bought bird treats formulated for parrots. Always ensure treats are given in moderation and do not exceed 10% of their daily intake. Avoid feeding table scraps or processed foods, as these can contain harmful ingredients.

3. Hydration: Fresh water is just as important as food. Ensure your conure always has access to clean, fresh water, and change it daily to prevent contamination. Avoid offering sugary or caffeinated beverages, as these are harmful to birds.

By paying attention to these details, you can tailor a diet that not only supports your conure's health but also adds enjoyment and variety to their daily life. Proper feeding practices are a cornerstone of responsible conure care and contribute to their happiness and longevity.

CHAPTER 5

TRAINING AND SOCIALIZING YOUR GREEN CHEEKED CONURE

Green-Cheeked Conures are intelligent, curious, and sociable birds that thrive when given proper training and socialization. Developing a positive relationship through consistent interaction not only improves your bird's behavior but also strengthens the bond between you and your feathered companion. With patience and the right techniques, training and socializing your conure can be a rewarding experience for both of you.

5.1 Basic Training Techniques

Training your Green-Cheeked Conure begins with understanding their natural behaviors and communication style. Use positive reinforcement and gentle methods to create a trusting relationship.

1. **Establish Trust**: Before formal training begins, ensure your conure feels safe and comfortable in your presence. Spend time near their cage, speak softly, and offer treats through the bars to build familiarity.

2. **Use Positive Reinforcement**: Reward desired behaviors with treats, praise, or gentle head

scratches. Avoid punishment, as it can damage trust and lead to fear or aggression.

3. **Start with Step-Up Training**:

   - Hold out your finger or a perch near your bird's feet and say "Step up" in a calm voice.
   - Gently nudge their belly if they hesitate and reward them immediately when they comply.
   - Repeat this daily until they consistently step up on command.

4. **Teach Target Training**:

   - Use a small stick or pointer and encourage your conure to touch it with their beak. Reward them when they do.
   - Target training is useful for directing your bird's movements and preparing them for more advanced tricks.

5. **Set a Routine**: Consistency is key. Short, frequent training sessions (5–10 minutes, 2–3 times a day) are more effective than lengthy ones.

5.2 Bonding and Socializing with Your Conure

Green-Cheeked Conures are naturally social and require daily interaction to stay happy and healthy. Building a strong bond involves trust, engagement, and understanding their needs.

1. **Daily Interaction**: Spend time with your conure outside their cage every day. Allow them to perch on your shoulder or hand while you go about your activities.

2. **Read Body Language**: Pay attention to their cues. For example, a fluffed-up bird may be content, while pinning eyes or an open beak

may indicate stress or irritation. Respect their boundaries to foster trust.

3. **Encourage Socialization with Others**: Introduce your conure to other family members gradually. This reduces dependence on a single person and promotes adaptability.

4. **Provide Mental Stimulation**: Engage your bird in foraging games, interactive play, or solving puzzles. This keeps their mind sharp and enhances their bond with you.

5. **Prevent Behavioral Issues**: Conures can develop habits like screaming or biting if they feel neglected or bored. Regular socialization and attention help mitigate these behaviors.

5.3 Teaching Fun Tricks and Vocalizations

Green-Cheeked Conures are quick learners and enjoy mastering new tricks or mimicking sounds. Training them to perform fun tricks or learn simple phrases can be both entertaining and enriching.

1. **Teach Simple Tricks**:

    - **Wave**: Encourage your conure to lift one foot by holding a treat near their feet and saying "Wave." Reward them when they perform the action.
    - **Turn Around**: Hold a treat in front of your bird and move it in a circular motion. As they follow the treat, say "Turn around" and reward them for completing the action.

2. **Encourage Vocalizations**:

    - Speak to your conure regularly and repeat simple phrases like "Hello" or "Good morning." Use an excited tone to catch their attention.

- Reward any attempt at mimicking sounds, even if they're not perfect. Conures may not be as talkative as larger parrots, but they can learn a few words or sounds over time.

3. **Combine Tricks and Cues**: Once your bird masters individual tricks, combine them into routines for added fun. For example, they can "step up" onto a stick, then "turn around" on command.

4. **Be Patient and Celebrate Progress**: Every conure learns at their own pace. Celebrate small milestones, and don't be discouraged if some tricks take longer to master.

Training and socializing your Green-Cheeked Conure is an ongoing process that requires patience, consistency, and understanding. By dedicating time to teach basic commands, encourage social behaviors, and introduce fun tricks, you'll nurture a deep and fulfilling bond with your bird. As you guide your conure through their learning journey, remember to approach every interaction with kindness and positivity, ensuring they thrive in your care.

CHAPTER 6

HEALTH AND WELL-BEING OF GREEN CHEEKED CONURES

Maintaining the health and well-being of your Green-Cheeked Conure is essential for their happiness and longevity. These vibrant and intelligent birds require attentive care, regular monitoring, and proactive efforts to ensure both physical and mental health. By understanding potential health concerns, adhering to preventative care routines, and providing daily enrichment, you can create a nurturing environment that allows your conure to thrive.

6.1 Common Health Issues and Symptoms

1. **Respiratory Problems**: Green-Cheeked Conures are susceptible to respiratory infections, often caused by drafts, poor ventilation, or exposure to irritants like smoke or strong chemicals. Symptoms include sneezing, wheezing, nasal discharge, and labored breathing. Prompt attention is necessary, as untreated respiratory issues can escalate quickly.

2. **Feather Plucking and Skin Irritation**: Stress, boredom, or underlying health issues may lead to feather plucking. This behavior, if not addressed, can result in skin infections or injuries. Monitor for signs such as bare patches, excessive preening, or visible wounds, and address both the physical and emotional causes.

3. **Nutritional Deficiencies**: A poor diet can lead to issues like vitamin A deficiency, which affects the respiratory and digestive systems. Signs of malnutrition include lethargy, a dull or flaky beak, brittle feathers, and decreased appetite. A balanced diet with fresh fruits, vegetables, and pellets is vital for their overall health.

4. **Psittacosis (Parrot Fever)**: This bacterial infection can cause lethargy, loss of appetite, green droppings, and respiratory distress. Psittacosis is also zoonotic, meaning it can

spread to humans, making immediate veterinary care crucial if suspected.

5. **Beak and Feather Disorders**: Conures are prone to overgrown or misaligned beaks, often due to a lack of natural chewing opportunities. Symptoms include difficulty eating or unusual beak growth. Provide bird-safe chewing toys and schedule regular beak trims if needed.

6.2 Regular Health Check-Ups and Preventative Care

1. **Annual Veterinary Visits**: Schedule yearly check-ups with an avian veterinarian to monitor your conure's overall health. These visits allow early detection of potential health issues and provide an opportunity to discuss diet, behavior, and general care.

2. **Vaccinations and Parasite Control**: While vaccinations are not always standard for conures, your veterinarian may recommend them based on regional risks. Regular checks for external parasites like mites or lice, and internal ones such as worms, are also essential.

3. **Maintain a Clean Environment**: Hygiene plays a critical role in preventing illnesses. Clean the cage daily, replace liners, and sanitize food and water dishes. Regularly disinfect perches and toys to minimize the risk of infections.

4. **Monitor Weight and Eating Habits**: Weigh your conure weekly using a small bird scale, as sudden weight changes can indicate illness. Observe their eating habits closely; a decrease in appetite, changes in droppings, or refusal to eat could signal an underlying problem.

5. **Avoiding Hazards**: Keep your bird away from household dangers such as non-stick cookware (which can release harmful fumes), toxic plants, or open water sources. Supervise them during out-of-cage time to ensure safety.

6.3 Ensuring Mental and Physical Stimulation

1. **Daily Interaction and Socialization**: Green-Cheeked Conures are highly social and require consistent interaction to stay mentally healthy. Spend time talking, playing, and training your bird daily to strengthen your bond and keep them engaged. Lack of socialization can lead to depression and behavioral problems like screaming or biting.

2. **Provide a Variety of Toys**: Offer an assortment of toys, such as foraging puzzles, chewable items, and interactive objects, to

encourage mental stimulation. Rotate toys regularly to maintain their interest and prevent boredom. Foraging activities mimic their natural behaviors and provide essential enrichment.

3. **Encourage Physical Exercise**: Conures are active birds that need opportunities to climb, flap, and explore. Install climbing nets, ropes, and swings in their cage. Provide supervised out-of-cage time daily, allowing them to stretch their wings and explore a safe environment.

4. **Establish a Routine**: Birds thrive on consistency. Set a daily schedule for feeding, playtime, and rest to create a sense of security. Ensure they get 10–12 hours of uninterrupted sleep each night by covering the cage or placing it in a quiet, dark room.

5. **Preventing Stress**: Stress can negatively impact both mental and physical health. Avoid

sudden changes in their environment, loud noises, or aggressive handling. If introducing new pets or people, do so gradually to prevent your bird from feeling threatened.

The health and well-being of your Green-Cheeked Conure depend on your diligence and dedication. By understanding common health issues, committing to regular preventative care, and providing mental and physical enrichment, you can ensure your conure leads a long, healthy, and joyful life. Remember, a happy and healthy bird reflects the care and attention they receive, making the effort you invest in their well-being immensely rewarding.

CHAPTER 7
BEHAVIORAL CHALLENGES AND SOLUTIONS

Understanding your Green Cheeked Conure's behavior is essential for fostering a positive relationship and ensuring their well-being. Like all pets, conures can exhibit behavioral challenges, ranging from minor annoyances to more serious issues. By recognizing these behaviors early and implementing appropriate solutions, you can create a harmonious environment for both you and your bird. In this section, we'll address common behavioral problems, ways to manage aggression and biting, and strategies for reducing stress in your conure.

7.1 Addressing Common Behavioral Problems

Behavioral issues are a normal part of owning any pet, and Green Cheeked Conures are no exception. Early intervention and consistent training are key to addressing these challenges and preventing them from escalating.

One common issue conure owners face is *excessive chewing*, especially on furniture, electrical cords, or cage bars. Chewing is a natural behavior for parrots, driven by both instinct and boredom. However, it can become problematic when they target inappropriate items. The solution is to provide plenty of chew toys made from bird-safe materials such as wood, paper, or cardboard. By redirecting their chewing behavior to appropriate toys, you satisfy their need for mental and physical stimulation.

Another challenge is *destructive behavior*, which often arises from a lack of environmental enrichment. Conures require a variety of toys, climbing structures, and perches to remain mentally stimulated. If these are missing, your bird may start to engage in destructive habits such as pulling out feathers, chewing on the cage, or dismantling furniture. Ensuring that your conure has an engaging and enriched environment is essential in preventing these behaviors.

Finally, *disregard for boundaries* can be a frustrating issue. Conures are curious and social creatures, but sometimes they can get too close for comfort, especially if they are not accustomed to being handled. Establishing boundaries through consistent training and positive reinforcement helps your conure understand what is acceptable behavior and fosters trust between you and your bird.

7.2 Handling Aggression, Biting, and Screaming

Aggression, biting, and screaming are behaviors that can be distressing for both owners and their birds. Understanding the underlying causes of these actions is crucial to managing them effectively.

Aggression and Biting: Green Cheeked Conures are known for their strong personalities, and aggression or biting can sometimes stem from fear, territoriality, or frustration. If your conure feels threatened or cornered, they may resort to biting as a defense mechanism. Additionally, if they are not getting enough mental stimulation or are overstimulated, they may bite out of frustration. To reduce aggression, it's important to spend time bonding with your bird and to avoid sudden movements or loud noises that may startle them. Consistently reinforce positive behavior through rewards, and use gentle handling to ensure they don't feel threatened.

If biting continues, consider providing more opportunities for foraging and interaction, which can reduce frustration. When handling your bird, always do so calmly, using a soft voice to assure them. Avoid punishment, as it can increase fear and aggression. Instead, redirect their attention to a toy or a safe space when they show signs of aggression.

Screaming: Screaming is a natural form of communication for conures, but it can become a nuisance if it's excessive. Conures may scream to get attention, express frustration, or communicate excitement. The best way to deal with this behavior is through consistency. When your conure screams, avoid reacting immediately, as this reinforces the behavior. Instead, wait for them to calm down before offering attention or a reward. If they scream for attention, you can redirect their focus with a toy or activity. It's also important to establish a routine for their meals, playtime, and sleep to reduce anxiety-driven vocalizations.

Consider the environment your bird is in—excessive screaming may also indicate a need for more environmental enrichment or social interaction. If your conure is alone for extended periods, they may become lonely or bored, leading to louder vocalizations.

7.3 Understanding and Managing Stress

Stress can be a major factor in the development of undesirable behaviors in Green Cheeked Conures. Birds are particularly sensitive to changes in their environment, and stress can manifest in a variety of ways, including feather plucking, excessive vocalization, or aggression.

Common Causes of Stress: Common stress triggers include sudden changes in the home, such as a new pet or person, relocation of the cage, loud noises, or changes in routine. Social birds like conures thrive on interaction, so a lack of attention or extended periods of isolation can lead to stress as well.

Managing Stress: To reduce stress, consistency and routine are crucial. Try to maintain a stable environment where your conure feels safe and secure. If there are changes in your home, introduce them gradually and provide plenty of reassurance to your bird.

Physical stress management is also important. Ensure your conure's cage is in a quiet, low-traffic area where they can retreat if feeling overwhelmed. Avoid loud noises or startling movements that might add to their anxiety. Additionally, engage your bird in daily activities, including playtime, foraging, and training, which can help alleviate stress and promote mental well-being.

If stress-related behaviors like feather plucking or aggression persist, consult with a veterinarian or an avian behaviorist. They can help assess whether there is an underlying medical issue or provide further training techniques to reduce stress.

By understanding the roots of aggression, biting, and screaming, as well as the signs of stress, you can address these challenges with patience, consistency, and the right strategies. With the proper management, your Green Cheeked Conure can thrive in a positive and stress-free environment.

CHAPTER 8

BREEDING AND RAISING GREEN CHEEKED CONURES

Breeding Green Cheeked Conures can be a rewarding experience, but it requires careful preparation, attention to detail, and a commitment to ensuring the health and well-being of both the parent birds and their offspring. This section will guide you through the process of preparing for breeding, caring for eggs and chicks, and raising healthy baby conures. Whether you're considering breeding as part of a conservation effort, or you simply want to understand the reproductive cycle of your birds, it's crucial to approach breeding with knowledge and responsibility.

8.1 Preparing for Breeding

Before embarking on breeding Green Cheeked Conures, it's essential to ensure that both the male and female are physically and mentally ready. Healthy, well-socialized birds with a stable temperament are more likely to breed successfully.

1. Choosing a Pair: Select a bonded pair of Green Cheeked Conures for breeding. Bonded pairs are typically more successful in reproduction as they already have a strong relationship. If you are introducing a new mate, give them time to get to know each other and develop a bond before breeding. Make sure both birds are of appropriate age (usually between 1 and 3 years old) and in optimal health.

2. Cage Setup: Create a comfortable and safe environment for breeding. Provide a spacious, quiet area where the birds can feel secure. Add a nesting box to the cage, as this will be crucial for the female to lay eggs. The nesting box should be large enough for the female to move around but small enough to provide a sense of security. Ensure the box is made from safe, natural materials and placed in a quiet, low-traffic area of the cage.

3. Diet and Health: Prior to breeding, ensure that both the male and female are on a balanced diet, rich in nutrients such as protein, vitamins, and minerals. Fresh fruits, vegetables, and high-quality pellets should be incorporated into their daily meals to ensure they are in peak condition for breeding. Supplement their diet with calcium, as this is essential for healthy egg production and overall reproductive health. Regular veterinary check-ups before breeding are important to rule out any underlying health issues that could affect fertility or the health of the chicks.

4. Timing and Seasonal Considerations: Green Cheeked Conures often breed in response to natural light cycles, typically during the spring and summer months when the days are longer. Adjusting the light in their environment to mimic seasonal changes can help trigger their natural breeding instincts. Provide them with 12-14 hours of daylight and a consistent, comfortable temperature.

8.2 Caring for Eggs and Chicks

Once the female has laid her eggs, the next step is to ensure proper care and protection. Egg incubation is a delicate process, and both parents must be involved for the best chance of success.

1. Incubation Process: Green Cheeked Conures usually lay between 3 to 6 eggs per clutch, with each egg being laid a day or two apart. After the final egg is laid, the female will incubate the eggs, while the male may assist by keeping watch and feeding her. If the parents are not incubating the eggs properly, you may need to intervene. In some cases, you might need to use an incubator, but this should only be done with caution and knowledge. The temperature of the incubator should be between 99-101°F (37.2-38.3°C), with a humidity level of around 55-65%. Ensure the eggs are rotated gently every few hours to prevent the embryos from sticking to the shell.

2. Egg Monitoring: Regularly check for signs of healthy development. The eggs should be firm and free from cracks. Candle the eggs every few days by shining a bright light through them to check for developing embryos. If an egg appears infertile or doesn't show signs of development after a week or two, remove it from the nest to avoid disturbing the rest of the eggs.

3. Hatching: The eggs will typically hatch in 23 to 30 days, depending on temperature and other conditions. When the chicks begin to hatch, the parents will continue to care for them, feeding them regurgitated food and keeping them warm. It's important to allow the parents to handle this part of the process as they have the natural instincts to care for their young.

8.3 Tips for Raising Healthy Baby Conures

Raising baby Green Cheeked Conures requires attention to detail and patience. Once the chicks hatch, the real work begins.

1. Feeding: During the first few weeks of life, baby conures rely on their parents for food, particularly regurgitated meals. If the parents are unable or unwilling to feed their chicks, you may need to step in and hand-feed them. Hand-feeding baby birds requires specialized formula and knowledge of the correct feeding techniques.

Consult with an avian vet or experienced breeder for guidance on how to hand-feed safely.

2. Growth and Development: Baby conures will grow quickly, developing feathers within a few weeks. By the time they are around 4 to 6 weeks old, they should start eating solid foods, including finely chopped fruits, vegetables, and pellets. Make sure to provide appropriate food at this stage, and gradually reduce the amount of hand-feeding as they begin to eat on their own.

3. Socialization: Socialization is a key part of raising a well-adjusted baby conure. Handle the chicks regularly from an early age to ensure they grow accustomed to human interaction. This will help them become more friendly, trusting, and comfortable around people once they are weaned. Gentle, positive interactions will help shape their behavior as they mature.

4. Weaning and Independence: As the chicks reach 8 to 10 weeks of age, they will begin to wean off their parents. Ensure that they have access to a variety of foods, including pellets, fruits, vegetables, and seeds, to encourage healthy eating habits. By the time they are 12 weeks old, most baby conures should be fully weaned and ready for their new homes or to stay with the parents if kept in the same aviary.

Raising healthy baby Green Cheeked Conures requires dedication and patience, but with the right preparation and care, you'll be rewarded with happy, healthy birds. Ensure they have a safe, enriching environment to grow and develop, and they'll become wonderful pets or breeders in the future.

CONCLUSION

In conclusion, Green Cheeked Conures are vibrant, affectionate, and intelligent birds that can make wonderful companions for those willing to invest time and effort into their care. From understanding their physical characteristics and unique personalities to creating an ideal living environment, providing a balanced diet, and addressing any behavioral challenges, each step in caring for these birds is essential to ensure their health and happiness. Whether you're interested in breeding, raising healthy chicks, or simply enjoying their lively companionship, a well-informed and committed approach is key to forming a strong, lasting bond with these delightful parrots. With the right environment, proper care, and attention, Green Cheeked Conures can thrive and bring joy to their owners for many years.

Printed in Great Britain
by Amazon